I AM NOT alone

FINDING PEACE IN GOD'S PRESENCE

A SOUL INSPIRED BIBLE STUDY

SWEET TO THE SOUL
ministries

I Am Not Alone —Finding Peace in God's Presence

A Soul Inspired Bible Study Booklet

Copyright © 2017 by Sweet To The Soul Ministries
All rights reserved.

www.SweetToTheSoul.com

ISBN-13: 978-1548190354

ISBN-10: 1548190357

Illustrations "jlk": Copyright © 2017 Jana Kennedy-Spicer

Cover Design by: Jana Kennedy-Spicer
Interior Design by: Jana Kennedy-Spicer

No part of this publication may be reproduced, distributed, or transmitted in any form or by any means, including photocopying, recording, or other electronic or mechanical methods, without the prior written permission of the publisher, except in the case of brief quotations embodied in critical reviews and certain other noncommercial uses permitted by copyright law. For inquiries and permission request, contact through website: www.SweetToTheSoul.com

Unless otherwise noted, all scripture quotations are taken from The Holy Bible, English Standard Version ("ESV®")
Copyright © 2001 by Crossway, a publishing ministry of Good News Publishers. Used by permission. All rights reserved. ESV Text Edition: 2011

Scripture quotations marked NIV are taken from The Holy Bible: NEW INTERNATIONAL VERSION, NIV Copyright © 1973, 1978, 1984, 2011 by Biblicia, Inc. Used by permission. All rights reserved worldwide.

Scripture quotations marked NASB are taken from the New American Standard Bible®, ("NASB") Copyright © 1960, 1962, 1963, 1968, 1971, 1972, 1973, 1975, 1977, 1995 by The Lockman Foundation Used by permission." (www.Lockman.org)

Scripture quotations marked NLT are taken from the Holy Bible, New Living Translation, copyright ©1996, 2004, 2007, 2013, 2015 by Tyndale House Foundation. Used by permission of Tyndale House Publishers, Inc., Carol Stream, Illinois 60188. All rights reserved.

CONTENTS

Introduction 1
Scripture Reading List 4
Joshua 1:9 Color Page 5
How to Use This Study 6

Section One

Scripture Pages 8
Zephaniah 3:17 Color Page 22
Blank Scripture Pages. 24
Prayer Journal Page 32
Deuteronomy 31:6 Color Page 33

Section Two

Loneliness Is A Lie. 34
Prayer Journal Page 38
Isaiah 43:19 Color Page 39
4 Ways to Break Loose from Loneliness 40
Prayer Journal Page 46
Color Page 47
The Blessing of Being Alone 48
Prayer Journal Page 52
1 John 5:14 Color Page 53

That's a Wrap 55
Meet The Authors 56
Proverbs 16:24 Color Page 57
Additional Resources 58

Sweet To The Soul Ministries

Harmony w/ my soul

God will be with them as their God
Revelations 21:3

LET YOUR Soul BE INSPIRED

God is a God of blessings.

God is a God of Promises Keeping

The stars are God's freckles!

Even though I walk through the shadow of death I will fear no evil.
Psalm 23:4

INTRODUCTION

Welcome to the Soul Inspired Bible Study - *I Am Not Alone : Finding Peace in God's Presence.*

Let me ask you a question. Have you ever felt alone?

I ask if you've *felt* alone, because I know you've *been* alone at some point. And the interesting thing about *feeling* alone is that it doesn't require actually *being* alone.

In fact, some of the times I have felt most alone I was surrounded by many people. Now days, because I work from home, I spend a lot of time by myself, but I rarely feel lonely when I am alone.

So if the feeling of loneliness isn't based on whether or not we are physically alone, *where does it come from*?

Think of a recent time when you felt alone? What were the circumstances?

Sweet To The Soul Ministries

For me, I think when the feelings of being alone creep in, they are prompted by feeling left out or not included, like I am missing out on something.

Many of my friends are attending an event this summer which I will not be attending. As I see them preparing and making plans I feel like the kid who stayed home while all their friends went to summer camp – *alone*.

But other times I have felt alone because of the circumstances I found myself, the particulars are not important, but I felt like no one else understood what I was going through. Because, in truth, no one in my circle had actually gone through the same experience, so I felt like *I was alone* in my crisis.

But God .... was present in the midst of both of these scenarios. *I was not alone.*

This is the truth that our Bible study is going to reveal and reinforce for us. Because as children of God, no matter the physical circumstances, no matter the emotional circumstances, we can all say – *I am not alone*. Because God says, "I am with you always."

"And behold, I am with you always, to the end of the age."
Matthew 28:20

My friend and fellow creative Liz Giertz from The Messy Desk is joining us in our study to share the truth about loneliness, ways we can break loose from loneliness and how we can find the blessing in being alone.

I so glad you are joining us on the Bible study journey because we are all in this together with a Heavenly Father who loves and never leaves us ... *we are not alone.*

Blessings Soul Friends,

So what are you hoping to learn or take away from this study?
Make a note of the situations which typically make you feel alone.

Sweet To The Soul Ministries

I AM NOT ALONE SCRIPTURES

31-DAY SOUL DEEP SCRIPTURE READING LIST:

1. Psalm 73:23
2. Deuteronomy 31:6
3. Isaiah 41:10
4. Zephaniah 3:17
5. Revelation 21:3
6. Matthew 28:20
7. Psalm 23:4
8. Joshua 1:9
9. Hebrews 13:5
10. Romans 8:38-39
11. 1 Corinthians 3:16
12. Revelation 3:20
13. John 14:16-17
14. Psalm 139:7-10
15. Ephesians 3:17
16. Joshua 1:5-6
17. John 14:23
18. Jeremiah 23:23-24
19. Matthew 18:20
20. John 10:27-30
21. Psalm 73:23
22. Exodus 33:14
23. Exodus 25:8
24. Isaiah 57:15
25. Judges 6:12
26. 1 John 1:7
27. 2 Corinthians 6:16
28. Psalm 91:1
29. Psalm 34:18
30. Psalm 145:18
31. Isaiah 43:2

Additional Scriptures:

1 Corinthians 14:25
Genesis 28:15
Leviticus 26:12

I Am Not Alone — Finding Peace in God's Presence

BE STRONG & OF Good Courage

JOSHUA 1:9

HOW TO USE THIS STUDY

In this study booklet, you have two sections.

In **SECTION ONE** you have a page for 7 of the scriptures on our reading list. Go at your own pace, whether a scripture a day or a week, or even several a day.

- On each scripture's page you'll see 5 sections.

READ : Read the scripture. Read it in context including the scriptures before and after, maybe even the whole chapter. Look it up in multiple translations. Then, write out the scripture in your own words, personalizing it specific to you and your current situation.

REFLECT : Use your Bible study sources (commentaries, dictionaries, etc or BibleHub.com) to learn more about the scripture. Make notations about what stood out to you.

RELATE : How does this scripture relate to you personally or your life situation? What does God want you to know from this scripture? How does it speak God's reassurances to you? Make all of these notations in this section.

REMEMBER : What is the one or main thing about the scripture which you want to remember?

PRAY : Conclude your study time by writing a prayer to God. Maybe incorporate portions of the scripture. Praise God and thank Him for the blessings in your life.

If you're like me, you may need more writing room, so keep some blank paper handy. Use the blank pages included to study additional scriptures.

In **SECTION TWO** you will find a devotional series by The Messy Desk's Liz Giertz.

There you will find three devotions to encourage you in the battle against loneliness.: Loneliness is a Lie, 4 Ways to Break Loose from Loneliness and The Blessing of Living Alone.

Included are several additional scriptures for study and reflections as well as some specific encouragements and challenges to help us win the battle against loneliness.

On the Prayer Journal pages, select one or two of the scriptures from each session to personalize and pray back to God.

Also you'll find lots of space to journal and let your soul be inspired.

FOR BIBLE JOURNALERS

Go to the scripture in your Journaling Bible and as you let your soul be inspired, journal about your study time.

I'd love to hear how God inspired your study time! Join us on Facebook or Instagram and share what you learned with us!

Sweet To The Soul Ministries

READ "Nevertheless, I am continually with you; you hold my right hand, you guide me with your counsel and afterward you will receive me to glory."

Psalm 73:23

REFLECT

RELATE

REMEMBER

PRAY

READ

"Be strong and courageous, do not be afraid or tremble at them, for the Lord your God is the one who goes with you. He will not fail or forsake you."

Deuteronomy 31:6

REFLECT

RELATE

REMEMBER

PRAY

READ

"Fear not, for I am with you, be not dismayed for I am your God; I will strengthen you, I will help you, I will uphold you with my righteous right hand."

Isaiah 41:10

REFLECT

I Am Not Alone —Finding Peace in God's Presence

RELATE

REMEMBER

PRAY

READ

"The Lord your God is in your midst, a mighty one who will save; he will rejoice over you with gladness; he will quiet you by his love; he will exult over you with loud singing."

Zephaniah 3:17

REFLECT

RELATE

REMEMBER

PRAY

READ "And I heard a loud voice from the throne saying, "Behold, the dwelling place of God is with man. He will dwell with them, and they will be his people, and God himself will be with them as their God." "

Revelation 21:3

REFLECT

RELATE

REMEMBER

PRAY

READ

"... And behold I am with you always, to the end of the age."

Matthew 28:20b

REFLECT

RELATE

REMEMBER

PRAY

READ   "Even though I walk through the valley of the shadow of death, I will fear no evil, for you are with me; your rod and your staff they comfort me."

Psalm 23:4

REFLECT

RELATE

REMEMBER

PRAY

he will rejoice over you with gladness

He Sings over me.

READ

REFLECT

RELATE

REMEMBER

PRAY

READ

REFLECT

RELATE

REMEMBER

PRAY

READ

REFLECT

RELATE

REMEMBER

PRAY

READ

REFLECT

RELATE

REMEMBER

PRAY

PRAYER JOURNAL

> DEUTERONOMY 31:6

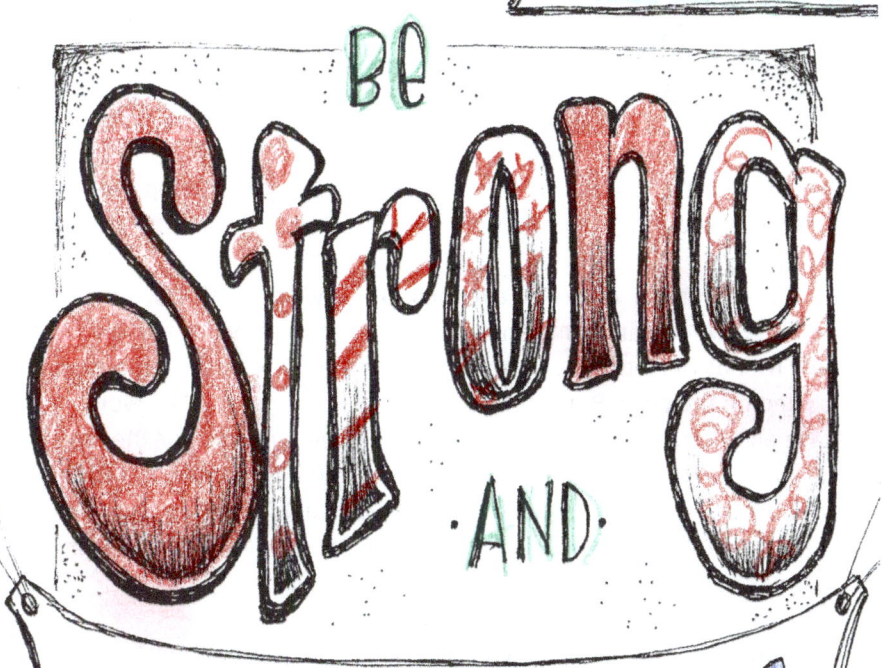

Be Strong AND Courageous

do not fear, the Lord goes with you.

LONELINESS IS A LIE

By: Liz Giertz

We are moving this summer and I'm preparing myself for a period of loneliness in our new location.

It's nothing new. I've moved every couple of years for the last two decades. We are an Army family. I've had a lot of practice making new friends once the boxes are all emptied and the packing material is piled on the curb. But this time already feels different. We won't have all the support systems I've grown dependent upon or the typical social circles where I am accustomed to finding my new friends. My husband might very well be the only active duty Soldier in the entire state of West Virginia. I'm going to be the new girl in a sea of civilians who probably won't understand our lifestyle.

The thought of being alone, feels like a curse to this extrovert.

The truth is lots of things can make us feel lonely. We don't have to move to a new state to feel isolated. Loneliness can even creep in when I'm in a crowded room. We can feel lonely when we are going through something nobody we know has experienced. Infertility. Miscarriage. Death of a child. Or a spouse. Or a parent. Enduring the absence of a prodigal. Suffering from an illness. Especially one that isn't visible. Divorce, depression, anxiety. Being a minority for any reason - ethnicity, gender, religion, or even age. There are a million different tricks the enemy of our souls employs to make us feel isolated. But they all boil down to one basic premise.

The sense of being unknown makes us feel alone.

But God's Word is full of reassurances for us. Here are a few of His promises I call on to combat the loneliness of feeling unknown.

Consider and notate how each of these scriptures can reaffirm that you are not alone.

HE SEES US.

"She [Hagar] gave this name to the Lord who spoke to her: "You are the God who sees me," for she said, "I have now seen the One who sees me." Genesis 16:13 NIV

HE HEARS US.

"This is the confidence we have in approaching God: that if we ask anything according to His will, He hears us." 1 John 5:14 NIV

HE KNOWS US better than we even know ourselves.

"You have searched me, Lord, and you know me. You know when I sit and when I rise: you perceive my thoughts from afar. You discern my going on and my lying down; you are familiar with all my ways."
Psalm 139:1-3 NIV

HE IS ALWAYS WITH US and will never leave or forsake us.

"Be strong and courageous. Do not be afraid or terrified because of them, for the Lord your God goes with you; He will never leave you nor forsake you." Deuteronomy 31:6 NIV

HIS SPIRIT RESIDES INSIDE US.

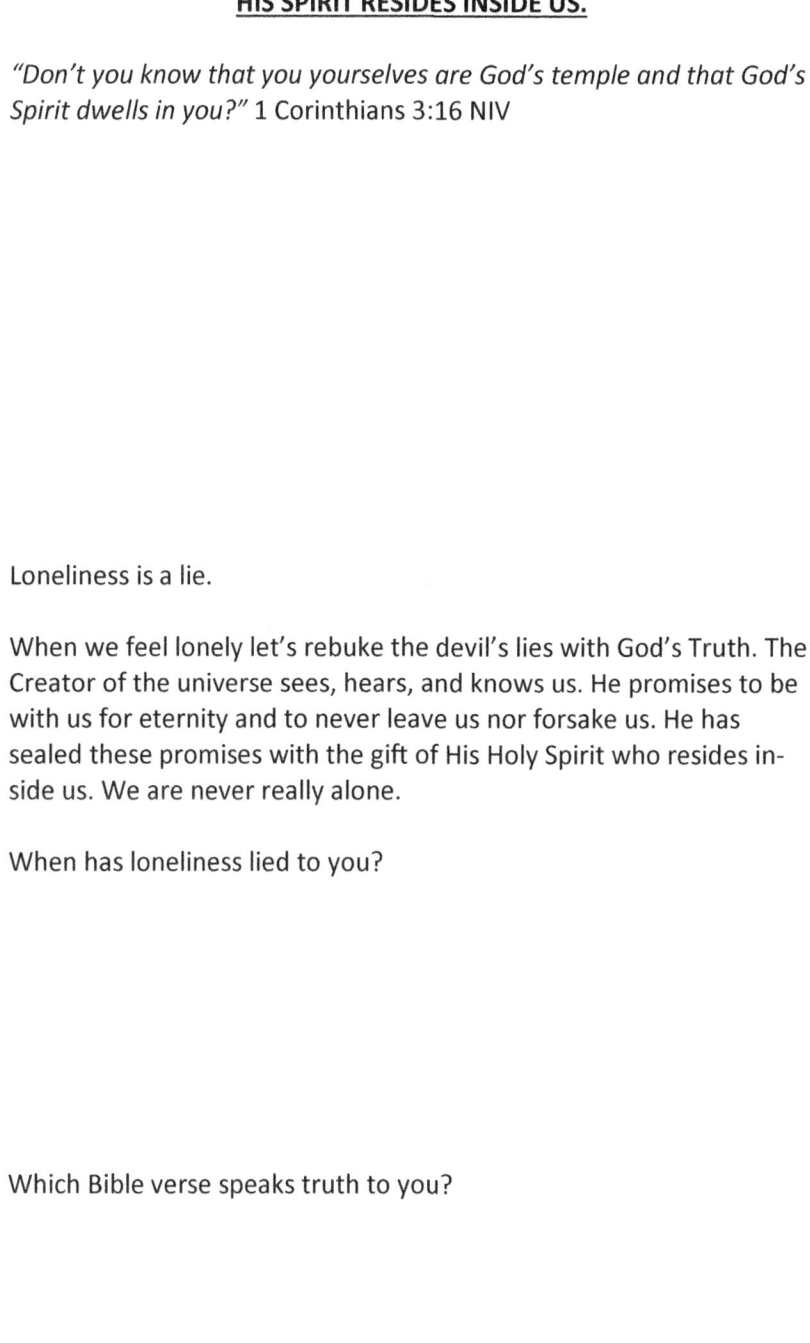

"Don't you know that you yourselves are God's temple and that God's Spirit dwells in you?" 1 Corinthians 3:16 NIV

Loneliness is a lie.

When we feel lonely let's rebuke the devil's lies with God's Truth. The Creator of the universe sees, hears, and knows us. He promises to be with us for eternity and to never leave us nor forsake us. He has sealed these promises with the gift of His Holy Spirit who resides inside us. We are never really alone.

When has loneliness lied to you?

Which Bible verse speaks truth to you?

PRAYER JOURNAL

ISAIAH 43:19a

now it Springs up; do you not perceive it?

4 WAYS TO BREAK LOOSE FROM LONELINESS

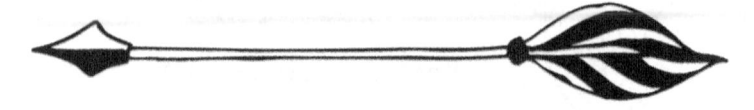

By: Liz Giertz

Knowing loneliness is a lie doesn't always keep it from latching on like an unwelcome party guest. Loneliness often creeps in during times of transition when I haven't connected with my community yet.

If loneliness is a lie and God's Word is truth, what do we do when our circumstances make us feel lonely?

It is rather pollyanna to think that just because I know the Truth about God's eternal presence in my life, I'll never feel alone. I often find my faith and my feelings in conflict. But just because I feel alone, doesn't mean my faith is faltering. We Christians need to arm ourselves with some practical solutions to fight back our feelings and break loose from loneliness.

When my feelings feed me a lie, I first fight back with the facts. I look to what God has already done to help me find the faith for what He will do in the future.

To find the courage to face the challenges looming on the horizon, I call on the MEMORIES. He has never left me lonely in any of our previous moves. In fact, it has been during times of transition that I have found Him closest. When I look to Him to comfort my aching heart, He has never let me down. The more I draw near to Him, the less alone I feel. He has always connected me to the community I crave, but sometimes it involves action on my part.

Here are four practical ways to break loose from lonely.

1. **LEAN into Him.** When there is nobody else to turn to, we have no choice but to lean on God. Times of loneliness may just be meant to drive us into the arms of our heavenly Father where we find eternal comfort and assurance.

"Trust in him at all times, O people; pour out your heart before him; God is a refuge for us." Psalm 62:8 ESV

BE INSPIRED: Pouring our heart out before God allows us to empty ourselves of, well, ourselves and makes room for God fill us back up with himself.
Write, pray or journal to God about what you are holding on to in your heart. Pour out what is in your heart, then spend time filling it back up with the truth in God's Word.

BIBLE JOURNALERS: .Journal Psalm 62:8, pouring out your heart to God

2. **LISTEN to His Word.** I would have used read, but it didn't fit with my "L" theme. The Bible is God's great love story to us. What better way to break loose from lonely than to be reminded how much we are loved by the creator of the universe.

"So faith comes from hearing, and hearing through the word of Christ." Romans 10:17 ESV

BE INSPIRED: We know that spending time in God's Word can provide the answer to our loneliness but often our days just do not allow the time to sit and read. But we can multitask and listen to the Word while we drive, walk or work.
Check out the variety of apps and on-line Bibles which you can listen to on-line or on devices and try them out.

BIBLE JOURNALERS: Select a scripture from pg XX and journal about how God inspires you through His Word.

3. **LOOK for what He is doing.** God is always at work here in this world. But often we are too busy to notice what He's doing. Sometimes we don't want to see how He is working things out for our good. Loneliness might just be a means to move us in a new direction, to give us a new perspective to see where He is working.

"See, I am doing a new thing! Now it springs up; do you not perceive it? I am making a way in the wilderness and streams in the wasteland." Isaiah 43:19 ESV

BE INSPIRED: Often we do not notice God working in our lives because our attention is focused elsewhere.
Take time today to carve out 10 to 15 minutes to specifically focus on what God has done in your life. Make a list or journal about a specific time when God worked out a situation in your life. Be reminded of his faithfulness.

BIBLE JOURNALERS: Review a journaled page in your Bible. Sit with God again recalling the learnings He has given.

4. **LOVE others the way He loves us.** When I feel lonely, I'm often looking for someone to love me - to notice and understand me and to accept and embrace me. It can be easy to forget God already does. Yet a desire to feel loved is one thing all man-kind craves. So perhaps giving love is the best way to get it back for ourselves. There is no greater way to connect with community than to go out and love others.

"A new commandment I give to you, that you love one another: just as I have loved you, you also are to love one another." John 13:34 ESV

BE INSPIRED: Loving others is something that we live out loud. So let's live it. Take notice of those around you this week and seek to meet someone's specific need.

BIBLE JOURNALERS: Join the challenge above, then select a scripture to journal about how God's love was shared with another.

The best way I've found to break loose from loneliness is lean in to God, listen to His Word, look for what He's doing and then go out and love others.

Which of these do you think would help you break loose from loneliness in your life? Under each, list a couple of ways you can incorporate the practice to help you battle loneliness?

1. **Lean into God**

2. **Listen to His Word**

3. **Look for What He's Doing**

4. **Go Out and Love Others**

Sweet To The Soul Ministries

PRAYER JOURNAL

LOVE one another

THE BLESSING OF BEING ALONE

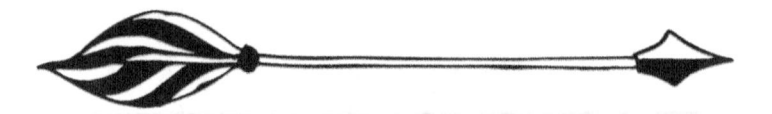

By: Liz Giertz

I'm an extrovert. I enjoy people. I consider a close connection with community to be one of life's greatest blessings. I gather women around My Messy Desk to craft each week to give them (and myself) a way to connect with each other.

So being alone can feel like a curse.

When things in this life feel like curses, I have to first remember Truth. God is a God of blessings and promise-keeping and working all things out for my good. Sometimes, I have to make a concerted effort to look for the good God is doing in the midst of my turmoil.

So why would God use my husband's reassignments to uproot me from my community every couple of years? Why would He leave me lonely? What could possibly be good about being alone?

At face value, being alone doesn't feel good. I know we were created to be in community with God and each other. But sometimes all the "each others" can get in the way of my connection with the Creator, even when my community is filled with fellow Christians. The longer I live in one place, the more community I connect with. After a while, commitments and responsibilities clutter my calendar and crowd out the sacred space I once reserved for connecting with God.

These things aren't necessarily bad in and of themselves. Most of them are good. Many of them are even necessary. Some of them are even God-appointed.

> *But when I'm drawing closer to my community than the Creator, I have a conflict.*

God has used all our moves in with the Army to drive home this important lesson.

Every time the Army issues new orders to my husband, I get to hit the reset button. There is a period of mourning the community we are leaving and some anxiety about getting connected in our new location. But for a few months at least I have a blank slate. I can use that time to feel lonely and sorry for myself, or I can look to see what God wants to do in my life, to see where He wants me to strengthen my connection with Him before I start building bonds in the community.

With fewer commitments I have more time for personal Bible study. With a cleaner calendar I have more pockets of time for prayer, more minutes to linger with the Lord, more room to rest and recharge, more space to be still and know. My immediate family may even get more of my attention than usual - whether they like it or not. And these are all very good things.

Let's stop looking at lonely like it's a curse and start believing in the blessings God longs to bestow upon us in times when we feel lonely.

First and foremost, God created us to be in communion with Him. He with His blessings. sent His Son to die for our sins so that sin couldn't sever that connection. Then, He gave us the blessing of community with each other. If we are all drawing closer to God, we are also all drawing closer to our eternal connection with each other in His kingdom.

The blessing of being lonely is discovering we are never really alone.

If you're feeling alone today, I urge you to use the time you might spend lamenting your lonely and look to God to fill those minutes with His blessings.

What are some things you can fill your lonely time with today? Make a list of the blessings you can enjoy when loneliness takes over.

Blessed

COUNT YOUR BLESSINGS

1

2

3

4

5

6

7

PRAYER JOURNAL

We have this **CONFIDENCE** toward **HIM** that if we ask anything according to His will He hears us.

· 1 JOHN 5:14 ·

THAT'S A WRAP

Soul Friends, it amazes me every time that when I finish one of the studies it is exactly the message I needed to hear from God. I realized that I feel lonely more often than I thought. But I also now have the reassurance from God that I am not alone.

And neither are you friend.

I know the scriptures I have studied here will be ones which I come back to time and time again. I have worked to memorize them so that when the enemy attacks and whispers the lies that I am alone or left out or not wanted, I can respond to his attack with the God's truth that He is with me always.

And thank you for taking this journey with me, Bible study may be quite personal, but there is joy in spending time with friends learning and talking about God's teachings.

As we go forward ...

Let's hold on to the truths from God's Word about His faithfulness and continue to pray with the expectation of God delivering an answer to those prayers.

Blessings Soul Friends,

Sweet To The Soul Ministries

MEET THE AUTHORS

Jana Kennedy-Spicer is a wife, mom and Nana who is passionate about inspiring and encouraging women on their daily walk with Christ. A woman rescued and repaired by the grace of God, she loves to share about the realness of God's love, redemption and faithfulness. Embarking on a new life journey, she is dedicated to using her blogging, Bible teaching, writing, photography, drawing, painting and graphic designs to bring glory to the Lord.

Jana teaches Bible Study and Bible Journaling in the Dallas, Texas area. To connect with Jana at www.SweetToTheSoul.com.

Holds my Hand

Liz Giertz. I am a U.S. Army combat Veteran turned Army wife and mother to two boisterous boys and one shelter pup (who provide endless content about overcoming messes). I enjoy quiet mornings spent with God while savoring a hot cup of sweet coffee...and if I can have those things with a beach view, all the better!

Along life's way, I stumbled through a whole bunch of messy stuff. But finding God's beauty underneath those scratches, dents, and dings is my most beloved discovery. That's why I'm passionate about connecting women through crafts and encouraging them to overcome their messes, embrace their memories, and become the masterpieces God created them to be. I'm still driven, but now I let God lead the way.

Connect with Liz at www.CreativeInspirationAtMyMessyDesk.com

Other Soul Deep Devotionals & Journals from *Sweet To The Soul Ministries*

31-Day Devotionals
Let Your Light Shine : Being a Light in a Dark World

31-Day Scripture Journals
New Life

Love Is

Grace

God's Masterpiece

I Believe

Let Your Light Shine

Everyday Thanksgiving

Anchored Hope

7-Day Scripture Journals
Together We're Better

Rest for the Weary Soul

Every Good Gift

For more information visit:
SweetToTheSoul.com/Soul-Deep-Books

Other Soul Inspired Products from
Sweet To The Soul Ministries

Coloring Books
Garden of Life
Love One Another
Bearing Fruit

Bible Study / Journaling Kits
Anchored Hope
Joy Filled Life
Bearing Fruit
Inspiring Women

Bible Journaling Templates / Color Your Own Bookmarks

Color Pages & Prints

Bible Journaling / Crafting Digital Kits
Gods' Masterpiece
Bearing Fruit

For more information visit:
SweetToTheSoul.com/Soul-Inspired

Or

Visit our Etsy shop at
www.etsy.com/shop/SweetToTheSoulShoppe

I am NOT ALONE

Made in the USA
Monee, IL
19 June 2022